Hallsc

A Village Betrayed

By STEVE MELIA

FOREST PUBLISHING

First published in 2002 by FOREST PUBLISHING, Woodstock, Liverton, Newton Abbot, Devon TQ12 6JJ

British Library Cataloguing in Publication Data

A catalogue record for this book is available from the British Library.

ISBN 0–9536852–4–1

Forest Publishing

Editorial, design and layout by:
Mike and Karen Lang

Typeset by:
Carnaby Typesetting, Torquay, Devon TQ1 1EG

Printed and bound in Great Britain by:
Wotton Printers Limited, Newton Abbot, Devon TQ12 4PJ

HALLSANDS – A VILLAGE BETRAYED

Introduction

During the night of January 26th 1917, at high tide, disaster struck the Devon fishing village of Hallsands as easterly gales lashed the roofs and walls of its stone cottages. Their terrified inhabitants watched helplessly, or clung to doorframes, as walls collapsed and floors fell away beneath them; whole families were trapped overnight in partially destroyed buildings hoping the tide would recede before the sea claimed what remained.

"This right of way has been removed by the sea and revoked by the Council", declares a sign alongside the coast path, with its majestic sweep over Start Bay. From the new viewing platform you can look down over the ruins – gable ends and chimney breasts on isolated outcrops of rock, towering over the sunken beach which used to support the village's only street. An information board refers to the story, which has fascinated generations of tourists and Devon schoolchildren, of Hallsands' demise. For this was more than a natural disaster; it is a story of man's interference with the balance of nature, a story of private greed and official incompetence. Its main characters are a shrewd businessman and politician, prevaricating civil servants, an engineer with a conscience, a determined local M.P. and a community of poor fishermen drawn into an unequal struggle.

The growing power of the press in mobilising public opinion was one sign of the changing times in which this story is set. The events were headline news at the time, and much has been written about them since, but the 'inside story' has remained largely concealed – until now.

Steve Melia
March 2002

Figure 1: The northernmost house of the village (*T.W. Barber*)

Figure 2: The central 'quays' in about 1900 (*Cookworthy Museum*)

4

Early Hallsands

Gaze over the ruins in winter today and you will appreciate what a harsh site this was for a village. Squeezed between the sea and the east-facing cliffs, plunged into shadows from early afternoon, no-one knows when or why people first decided to settle there, but the same family names recur in records and censuses across the generations; the Trouts, the Prettejohns and the Lynns, both in Hallsands and Beesands (its sister village a couple of miles north along the coast).The earliest records mention a "Chapel of the Blessed Virgin Mary" at Stert (Start Point today), which was already "quite ancient" by 1507. Today no traces remain to suggest where it might have stood, but the Stokenham Manor Rolls in the early 17th century refer to a "Halesande Chapell at Halsands" and a "fishing howse at Halesands".

The first houses were built on exposed rock and compacted sand, with some, such as figure 1, ingeniously built against, or into, the rock. As the population grew during the 19th century (from 106 in 1851 to 159 – in 37 dwellings – by 1891) other houses were built on the seaward side of the village's only street, their foundations being laid on platforms of shingle extending across the beach to low walls, known as the 'quays'. Behind its quays and its pebble beach, the village withstood all the storms and high seas of the 19th century. Even the terrible storms of 1891 caused "only such minor damages as a few loose slates".

In 1857, on the death of Sir Robert Newman, the houses were offered for sale to their tenants. How they raised the money to buy their houses is not recorded, but from that time on Hallsands became a village of modest owner-occupiers. In an age when renting from private landlords was more common than today, this change was to have important implications. For the villagers, their precarious homes were their main assets, a compelling reason to stay and fight: but a threat to the village was no longer a threat to powerful interests.

Life at Hallsands before the storm

From its earliest times fishing was the life of Hallsands. Apart from a few agricultural labourers and the coastguard station, every household depended to some extent on fishing. Lacking the harbour to support a trawler fleet, the Hallsands fishermen specialised in inshore crab fishing, or 'potting'. It was a complicated business, starting with crab pots made of willow, catching of bait in two stages, then setting, checking and hauling in the pots. The complexity of the work required the co-operation of nearly everyone in the village, their sense of community strengthened by their dependence on each other. The first stage of the fishing for bait used huge 'seine' nets, rowed out for up to a mile

Figure 3: Seine netting at Hallsands, 1951 (*Norman*)

with the opposite ends remaining on shore. The whole village would help haul these nets back in to shore, each man receiving one share of the catch with a two-thirds share for each woman and three shares going to the owner of the boat and net. Tourists watching the hauling-in would sometimes comment that the women on shore seemed to have a harder job than the men, who would go into the water as the net approached to prevent the fish from escaping. As Frederick Steer, a fisherman from neighbouring Beesands, explained:–

"We always kept a Seine net in a boat on the beach ready in case a school of fish such as mullet or mackerel came along. A man on the look-out would be on the cliff top to spot these fish and would give a loud whistle to warn the fishermen to put the boat out. They would all shout 'Hey boat!'. You would see the men and women rush from all directions. The pub would empty out. They were all there to help the net in."

Fish such as mullet and mackerel were too soft for crab bait so some of these catches were taken by horse and trap to the nearest railway station, seven miles away at Kingsbridge, or bought by hawkers who would sell them around the local farms. Some were kept for the fishermen's families and the rest were used as bait by three- or four-man boats trailing 'longlines' to catch firmer fish like gurnards, used as bait for the crab pots. Both the smaller crab boats and the larger ones employed for seine netting used sail and oar, and again all hands (including women) were needed to haul the boats in. Figures 4 and 5 illustrate the importance of the pebble beach to the fishermen: for beaching boats, stacking pots and drying nets.

In the days before radios and life-jackets, fishing was a hazardous business – there were many incidents of boats lost at sea and fishermen rescued from the water by the crews of other boats. Surprising though it may seem, most of the fishermen were unable to swim.

The crabs and lobsters were taken to Kingsbridge railway station or

Figure 4: Hallsands from the south, 1894 (*R. Hansford Worth*)

Figure 5: Net drying lines by the southern slipway (*Cookworthy Museum*)

Figure 6: Fishermen waiting for the tide (*Cookworthy Museum*)

Figure 7: From left – Bill Login, Mrs Lynn, Mr Lynn, Georgie Steer, George Stone, Bob Trout (bowler hat), Wilf Login, Cyril Stone, John Login, George Stumbles, Jack Steer, Jack Trout and Jim Lynn (foreground weaving pot) (*Cookworthy Museum*)

sometimes kept alive in bigger storage pots to be picked up by a 'crab smack', a sailing boat which came from Southampton every week or two. The arrival of this boat could never be predicted and crabs would sometimes deteriorate during the wait. Ultimately, much of the fish was sold at Billingsgate market, in London, from where the buyers would telegraph the crew to tell them how much the catch had brought. It was a risky business: if a catch was rejected the crew could be left with a bill for its carriage. Stephen Reynolds, a 'gentleman' who spent several years living with fishermen further up the coast at Sidmouth, explained:–

"It is ashore that the fisherman comes off worst of all. Neither educated nor commercialised, he is fleeced by the buyers. Dick Yeo once went up to Billingsgate and saw his own fish sold for about ten pounds. On his return ... he received three pounds odd, and a letter from the salesman to say that there had been a sudden glut in the market."

In his book *A Poor Man's House*, Reynolds was struck by the skill of the women in managing the family budgets when all fishing ceased for weeks, or even months, at a time during winter. At these times the fishermen would cut willow, used to make their crab pots, from nearby groves, repaying the farmers with their labour, or fish. Some of the fishermen would also work on the farms at different times of the year in order to supplement their income.

Bad weather and sharp practice by the fish buyers were not the only threats to the Hallsands fishermen. Trawling within three miles of the shore in Start Bay was prohibited by a bylaw which the inshore fishermen would often accuse the Brixham trawlers of flouting. The Devon Sea Fisheries Committee became a forum for conflict between the two groups, occasionally taking enforcement action against trawler skippers, who were caught and, sometimes, jailed. Simmering hostility between the two groups culminated in 1925 with an incident where shots were fired at the Hallsands fishermen (and one fisherwoman) as they confronted a trawler fishing illegally at night with lights extinguished – fortunately, it seems, no-one was hit. These conflicts, which continued over several decades, underlined the vulnerability of the inshore fishermen; unlike the trawlers, they had nowhere else to go.

We know fishing families in Beesands kept chickens, ducks and pigs to supplement their diet, and old photographs, such as figure 8, show fowl along the narrow street of Hallsands, but space would not have permitted the keeping of many larger animals. Flotsam found on the beach was a welcome bonus: driftwood for household fires, soap and, on one occasion, candles, which were particularly useful as there was no electricity in the village. On another occasion a barrel of brandy was washed ashore. Unused to hard liquor, it seems several of the men drank to excess, and one poor soul was found dead shortly afterwards.

There was one pub in the village (the London Inn), a post office and one grocer/baker, whose supplies were brought in by pony and trap from

Figure 8: Chickens supplemented the diet of many families (*By kind permission of Fred Lynn*)

Figure 9: The village post office (*Cookworthy Museum*)

Kingsbridge. The butcher from Torcross, along the coast, would deliver twice a week by horse and cart across the beach at low tide, and children used to collect milk and butter from nearby farms. Reminiscing about her childhood many years later, Edith Patey described life in Hallsands as follows:–

"We all felt in those days one big happy family. When everyone was 'in the same boat' so to speak. We were all humble and poor people. Sharing was uppermost in village life. Thoughts were living things, our faith was made stronger."

Non-conformist religions were strong in the Westcountry at that time; the little white Bible Christian Chapel on the cliff top overlooking the village was well attended, and also ran a Sunday school for the children. A reading room, which was to be of growing importance as events unfolded, provided a venue for concerts and meetings.

Formal education for ordinary people came to the area in 1877 with the building of a local board school at Huckham. The Hallsands children would walk the two miles or so inland to attend, from the age of five until thirteen or fourteen. Teaching the children of working-class families to read and write was a key aim of the 1891 Education Act, which made these schools free and compulsory, but progress in places like Hallsands was slow. By 1904, when eighteen villagers were presented with a document of vital importance to our story, six were unable to sign their own name.

Figure 10: The northern end of the village, showing the Bible Christian Chapel (*R. Hansford Worth*)

Sir John Jackson and the Keyham contract

Some 25 miles north-west of Hallsands lies Devonport, built around the naval dockyard that it was founded to serve and, at that time, the second largest town in Devon. As the size of ships grew towards the end of the 19th century the Admiralty decided to extend the docks, doubling them in size. At least six companies were invited to tender for the work, and in January 1896 the contract was awarded to Sir John Jackson Ltd.

At the age of 45 Sir John was the owner of one of the biggest civil engineering companies in the country. Son of a goldsmith, he had studied engineering at Edinburgh and had obtained the contract to build Stobcross Docks in Glasgow at the age of just 25. His performance there had established his "reputation for smartness and thoroughness" and for completing contracts

Figure 11: The Keyham dock extension nearing completion (*Plymouth Museum*)

ahead of schedule. Knighted for his work on the Manchester Ship Canal, he concentrated on large public contracts in Britain and its colonies.

Shortly after winning the Keyham contract, Sir John moved to Devonport and, despite the scale of his work commitment, immediately threw himself into politics. During the previous year the Conservative/Unionist coalition had replaced the Liberal Party in Government and Sir John, seeing an opportunity, put himself forward as Conservative candidate for the county council, to which he was elected in November 1896. It was the first step in a parallel career that was to see him elected as M.P. for the town in 1910. Referring to a building project which he opposed, his election leaflet said:–

"I am opposed to putting large sums of money into the pockets of some of the ratepayers. I shall always, if it occurs, protest against any member of a public body taking advantage of his official position, in endeavouring to get land or properties and re-selling the same to the Town."

He was also a lay preacher, fond of delivering homilies to his workforce, such as this one in 1905:–

"...if they wished, as all patriots must, that this good old country should retain its record for honest work, straightforwardness, commercial morality, and piety, their first thought must be truth, charity and character."

These are interesting words in view of his later actions. Although we have

13

PLYMOUTH COUNTY COUNCIL.

ST. PETER'S WARD.

Yours faithfully,

J. G. JACKSON.

Figure 12: Sir John Jackson's election leaflet (*Plymouth Records Office*)

no direct evidence of corruption against Sir John, his political influence and wealth grew along with his success in obtaining public contracts, sometimes on particularly favourable terms.

He was resourceful in solving problems and cutting costs; when a shortage of Cornish granite threatened his work at Keyham, he began importing the stone from Norway. The vast areas of concrete involved in the new dock posed another problem – how to obtain shingle at the lowest cost. Offshore dredging seemed to offer the cheapest solution, if a suitable site could be found.

His first application to dredge was addressed to Exeter Corporation, which controlled the navigation rights in the Exe estuary. Unlike Hallsands, however, most of the town of Exmouth was owned by a powerful landowner: the Hon. Mark Rolle, a significant contributor to the funds of the Conservative Party in Devon. In December 1896 Rolle's solicitors wrote to the Board of Trade expressing concern that the "considerable scale" of Sir John's plans "might seriously damage Exmouth". "Unable to obtain a definite reply" from Rolle, and presumably unwilling to upset him, Sir John decided to halt his dredging in the Exe and move his plant further down the coast to Dartmouth.

In August 1896, Sir John had asked the Board of Trade for permission to extract shingle from along the coast between Hallsands and neighbouring Beesands. His letter says:–

"The quantity required cannot be accurately stated but in no case will it be sufficient as to in any way interfere with the cliffs or adjoining land and to satisfy you in this respect I have already obtained the consent of the adjoining landowner."

The landowner, a Mr Cole of nearby Kellaton, owned a stretch of the coast from just beneath the Christian Bible Chapel to Tinsey Head, as shown on figure 13. Figure 14 shows how close the chapel was to the northern end of the village and the beach on which the fishermen depended.

The shingle was the property of the Crown, under the control of the Board of Trade (below low water mark) and the Office of Woods (above low water). Officials at the Board of Trade initially considered a payment of two pence per ton; then, for reasons which are unclear, Sir John was offered an alternative to pay a flat rate. Over the five years dredging was permitted, Sir John's company was to pay just £1,000 for the privilege, with no obligation to account for the quantities of shingle removed. Later estimates vary widely, but it seems the original proposal would have yielded the Government between four and twenty times this amount.

Apart from confirming this highly favourable term, the Agreement included a clause giving the Board of Trade the right to cancel the licence if they believed the operations "may in any way damage the foreshore defences of the adjacent district". At no stage does it seem that the villagers were consulted or even informed.

Many years later Sir John was to reveal a curious conversation with his solicitor, who suggested the company "might purchase the whole of Hallsands

Figure 13: Part of the 1885 O.S. map, reproduced at a scale of 3.6 inches to one statute mile

Village". The ostensible reason for this suggestion, which was not pursued, was provide accommodation for company workers. Was this the only reason, or was Sir John (or his advisors) aware of the likely consequences of his plans?

Figure 14: The dredging started directly below the chapel (right) (*Cookworthy Museum*)

The dredging begins

In April 1897, with the villagers still unaware of what had been agreed, dredgers like the one shown in figure 15 appeared off the shore immediately north of the village. As a later account was to put it:–
   "The greater part of the shingle was taken between high and low water mark, so that the dredgers sucked the very beach itself."
   Horrified by what they saw, the villagers turned to their representatives for help. Putting its divisions aside, the Devon Sea Fisheries Committee called on the Board of Trade to halt the dredging until an inquiry could be held. The villagers were also to find a powerful ally in their M.P., Frank Mildmay, heir to the nearby Flete Estate and another in Shoreham, Kent. Educated at Eton and Cambridge, he had trained as a barrister before winning the Totnes Constituency for the Liberal Party in 1885. Then, a year later, he had followed the Liberal Unionists who broke away from Gladstone's party over the issue of Irish home rule and formed a coalition with the Conservatives – the party of Sir John Jackson, who he always treated with a gentleman's courtesy

Figure 15: The only remaining picture of one of the dredgers (*The Devonshire Association*)

Figure 16: Frank Mildmay M.P. (*Guy Pannell*)

throughout the toughest of negotiations. Now, after twelve years in Parliament, had established a reputation as a conscientious, hard-working M.P. As a biographer of his family was to put it: "he always had the deep sense of responsibility of one born to great possessions". And he had already endeared himself to the fishermen of Hallsands with a solution to one of their most challenging problems – the hazards of landing the boats in high surf – with a gift of several dogs, trained to swim ashore with ropes in their mouths.

The first inquiry

On May 13th 1897 Mildmay addressed a parliamentary question to the President of the Board of Trade, C. T. Ritchie, asking "whether he will hold a local inquiry upon the allegations as to the damage to fishermen's cottages and from the fishing industry likely to result therefrom…". In his reply, Ritchie claimed credit for the clause in Sir John's contract, allowing for its cancellation in case of damage. Ignoring Mildmay's call for a moratorium in the meantime, he agreed to the main request, appointing the Hon. Capt. Vereker as inspector.

Figure 17: Hallsands before the dredging. Note the coastguard station, top centre (*Fred Lynn*)

The inquiry was arranged for June 1897, in the coastguard station overlooking the village. The villagers were represented by three of the fishermen and Edward Windeatt, a Totnes solicitor and election agent to Mildmay. Sir John Jackson Limited, the Devon Sea Fisheries Committee and the coastguards were also all represented. Windeatt opened for the fishermen, explaining how noise and disruption caused by the dredgers had cost the fishermen as much as £150 in lost catches of mullet and mackerel over the last season. And a south-easterly storm, he feared, would carry the shingle away from the village to fill the excavations made by the dredgers. George Wills spoke for the fishermen who were "unanimously opposed" to the dredging. The beach, he said, was a shifting one and if large quantities of it were taken away there was a "great risk" that their houses would be "carried away by a storm".

Sir John Jackson himself did not attend, but the arguments of his representatives were to set the tone for a debate that would rage for years to come. Acknowledging the disruption to fishing, they offered to halt the dredging "if given notice of fish in the bay" (how much "notice" they expected from shoals of fish was not reported!). With no hint of irony, they explained that attempts to dredge at Exmouth had been abandoned following "objections", leaving this stretch of coast as their only alternative. The owner of the land behind the shore had given his permission and, in any case, the sea would replenish whatever was taken. To this, one of the fishermen replied:

Figure 18: The village, from the beach, in about 1900 (*Cookworthy Museum*)

20

"what Sir John Jackson takes down to Devonport can never come back again".

Capt. Vereker's report, along with many of the earlier documents, has disappeared from the Government's files, but the Board's response can still be found at the Public Record Office in Kew. In July 1897 T. H. Pelham, Assistant Secretary for Fisheries, wrote to Frank Mildmay saying the Board had considered the report, concluding the operations "will not cause any damage to the beach or houses", although he listed three concessions offered by Sir John's company. The dredging operations would move northwards, further from the village; they would stop when requested during netting; and the company would pay for any loss of crab pots or buoys. This evidently failed to convince the fishermen and negotiations continued through Mr Windeatt, resulting in a further offer of £125 a year, to which Sir John later added a "Christmas gratuity" of £20. This amounted to £1 10s a year for each fisherman (around £100 at today's prices) and £1 2s 6d for each fisherwoman. Smaller payments were also made to the fishermen of Beesands. Despite their misgivings, the fishermen had little choice but to accept, so the dredging continued through three years of uneasy truce.

First signs of damage

Around 1900 the passing visitor to Hallsands would have noticed little change in the beach, but the fishermen who knew it best could see that its level was beginning to fall. As the months passed they saw the high tides approaching a little closer to their houses. Storms, which would have spent their force on the shingle ridge in the past, were now lashing the walls and foundations on the seaward side of the road. The London Inn, built over rock and sea wall was one of the first buildings to suffer. In November 1900 its owner, Mr Spital, took the initiative with a memorial signed by fishermen and householders complaining to the Board of Trade about damage to their property. The Board passed this to Sir John Jackson for his "observations" and asked the coastguard to comment on the state of the beach. Later papers found in the Board's files reveal a strange response from the coastguard: the beach had indeed fallen below high water mark but was unchanged above it. They confirmed some of the houses had been "affected by Southerly gales" but doubted whether the dredging was to blame. Sir John, typically, responded by denying all responsibility but offering a concession:–

"that in the event of any damage being done by ordinary gales or tides during our work, or within six months after we have ceased…we will make good such damage to the village or shore buildings if attributable to our works".

With this ambiguous offer, the Board replied to Mr Spital denying "the memorialists have shown any sufficient ground of complaint". The villagers do not appear to have replied to this letter, but they were to invoke Sir John's offer a few months later.

In March 1901 the Board received what one civil servant described as "a long and very intemperate letter" from Mr Spital. He had reason to be annoyed: along the length of the village, and beneath his inn, the quay walls had been undermined. Sir John's company made some limited repairs "without prejudice" and also offered to buy some of the damaged properties. Advised by his solicitor before the dredging began, we know Sir John believed the whole village to be worth no more than £1,500. Based on the purchase price of a couple of cottages in 1902, the true value would have been more than double this level, so his offers were probably less than generous – it seems none was accepted.

The authorities might have continued to ignore the growing damage to private houses were it not for the deterioration of the coastal road. In February 1901 Messrs Harris & Sons, the grocers from Kingsbridge who supplied the village by pony and trap, wrote to Kingsbridge Rural District Council complaining of "the dangerous state of the road" between Hallsands and Beesands. They also threatened to hold the council liable for any damage to their vehicles. The council responded by appointing a committee who examined the road and agreed the stretch in front of the chapel was now dangerously close to the edge of the cliff. They decided to move the road back, calling the attention of Sir John Jackson Ltd and the Commissioner of Woods and Forests to the damage which they believed to be related to the dredging. The commissioner then replied to this by enclosing an "independent" report commissioned by Sir John, which agreed that the damage was serious but claimed "there was not the slightest indication that the removal of shingle would in any way affect" the road. The district council, in turn, forwarded this report to Stokenham Parish Council, which was clearly unimpressed: instead, it protested against "the destruction of the beach from Hallsands to Beesands by the dredging" and suggested a new road be built further inland. But it seems these calls were to have little impact on the civil servants at the Board of Trade – an entry in their files refers to a report, now lost, with a note saying simply "do not propose to take any action"!

The brief (and in places disintegrating) minute books of these periods betray a difference in attitude between the two local authorities. The parish council, influenced by the vicar of Stokenham, did at least show signs of sympathy for the villagers, although its powers were limited. The district council, with greater resources and influence, on the other hand, was to show little sympathy and an overriding determination to avoid any costs falling on itself.

Until this time the issue had received scant coverage in the press; then, in May 1901, an unnamed reporter from the Plymouth *Western Daily Mercury* visited Hallsands and wrote an article headed 'Devon Fishing Village in Peril'. After examining marks on the rocks, he confirmed the beach had fallen six, seven "even fifteen feet in places", with terrible consequences for the fishermen. Whereas the shingle ridge had provided a safe resting place in all weathers, "now with a slight freshening breeze it is necessary to remove all the boats to the roadway...Consequently, the men dread to contemplate the havoc which a S.E. gale would play in winter".

The report hints at the fatalism which was often to mark the villagers' reaction to their plight, concluding with the words:–

"The fishermen are unanimously of the opinion that the beach will not come back. Where has it gone? 'Way down Plymouth' was the repeated response, whoever was asked."

Confrontation

With no sign of any concession from the civil servants, Mildmay approached the Earl of Dudley, Under Secretary at the Board of Trade. In July 1901 he was able to forward to Kingsbridge Rural District Council an offer from the earl to appoint an "expert" to report on the situation. At around the same time the *Western Daily Mercury* again sent a reporter to Hallsands to interview the villagers. The news of another inspection was greeted with general scepticism, as the last one had made so little difference. To illustrate how far the beach had dropped Mr Spital, owner of the London Inn, pointed out a wall where "people used to play capers with a donkey and make him jump it", the seaward side

Figure 19: Wilson's Rock, 1894 (*Messrs Valentine*)

Figure 20: Wilson's Rock, 1902 (*E. Croft*)

being only slightly lower. "At the present time on the seaward side of the wall, there is a drop of nearly fifteen feet, enough to kill any donkey who took the wall now!"

On September 11th 1901 Capt. G. C. Frederick, appointed by the Board, visited Start Bay to interview local witnesses and examine the three miles or so of coast from south of Hallsands to Torcross in the north. By examining marks on rocks, he concluded the level of the beach had fallen along the whole coast. At the stretch where the dredgers were operating between Hallsands and Beesands the level had fallen by up to 12 feet. Figures 19 and 20 show how the beach at the northern end of the village receded between 1894 and 1902, revealing Wilson's Rock, which had scarcely protruded above the sand before dredging began. In his report, received by the Board on September 19th 1901, Capt. Frederick posed three questions:–

1. Would the continuance of dredging endanger or seriously affect the houses in the villages of Hallsands and Beesands?
2. Does the dredging seriously interfere with the fishing industry carried on by the inhabitants of these villages?
3. Is the erosion of the beach caused by dredging likely to endanger the public road between Hallsands and Beesands?

To answer the third question, he inspected the shore between Hallsands and Tinsey Head, where "the beach has been so denuded of shingle that large rocks are appearing". Figure 21, taken in front of the village a couple of years later, illustrates the problem, although figure 22, taken from the same spot in August 1901, shows that the worst effects were yet to hit the village itself. "At the time of my visit", he comments, "a labourer in the employ of Sir John Jackson was

Figure 21: The centre of the village in October 1903 (*R. Hansford Worth*)

Figure 22: The centre of the village in August 1901 (*R. Hansford Worth*)

engaged in breaking up these stones, as according to his statement they are drawn down to the holes made by the dredger and block the suction pipe". This "denudation of the beach has allowed the sea to wash the softer material away and efface the road...if dredging continues it is only a matter of time before the road is washed away".

His answer to the second question was equally emphatic:–

"There is no doubt whatever that the dredging operations seriously interfere with the fishing industry. The presence of the dredger, tugs and barges...are especially detrimental to seine fishing: while in consequence of the destruction of the beach...the seines can only be hauled at considerable risk on account of the large rocks and stones left exposed."

Referring to the compensation paid by Sir John since 1897, he points out that at the time little damage had occurred to the beach and that it "cannot be considered to err on the side of generosity".

In front of the village the spring tides now came within 30 feet of the sea wall, so "with a fresh inshore wind the sea washes over this narrow strip...deluging the houses with spray; and in the event of a heavy gale from the eastwards direction I should think there will be few houses that will not be flooded, if not seriously damaged". With these unequivocal answers, and acknowledging Sir John's contract at Devonport still had some time to run, he concluded his report with a recommendation "that further dredging in this vicinity should be discontinued".

In keeping with their accommodating attitude towards Sir John, the Board did not act immediately but privately forwarded a copy to his solicitors for "your client's observations". The Board was evidently uncomfortable with the implications of Capt. Frederick's conclusions (if the dredging was threatening the village, then who would be liable for any damage?). Frank Mildmay was the only other person allowed to view a copy "under a vow of secrecy", which prevented even the local authorities from seeing it. Faced with this threat to his operations, Sir John's first reaction was to request a delay to consider his response. The Board agreed to give him a month, until October 25th, during which time no more than 10,000 tons of shingle was to be removed. Two days before this deadline his solicitors wrote to the Board offering to re-open negotiations with "all parties interested", provided the dredging was allowed to continue in the meantime. The Board agreed, on condition that no more than one dredger was to operate at a time. We have no record of these negotiations but we know their outcome – whatever Sir John offered failed to move the villagers, by now implacably opposed to dredging on any terms.

Over the years, several observers were to comment on the great restraint shown by the villagers in the face of these terrible events. But at the end of 1901, three months after Capt. Frederick's inspection, and with no sign of an end to the dredging, the patience of the fishermen finally expired. On New Year's Day 1902 the men of Hallsands left the village together and walked along the crumbling road to Beesands. At its opposite end, united by ties of blood, the sea and a common threat, the men of Beesands were marching to meet them. They then came together on the mooring jetty at Greenstraight, to confront the dredgers. Did their anger turn to violence or did Sir John's employees retire, gracefully, or intimidated? The brief accounts remaining do not tell us, but whatever was said or done the dredgers withdrew, never to return to that stretch of coast.

In fact, unbeknown to the villagers, the Board of Trade had decided, on the previous day, to revoke the licence with effect from January 8th. So, with dredging brought to an end, the villagers may have believed that their ordeal was over, but they were to discover the worst was yet to come.

Outside the law?

Unwilling to accept defeat, Sir John instructed his solicitors to write to the Board of Trade challenging its "arbitrary" decision to revoke the licence. They acknowledged for the first time that dredging above low water mark might have caused some damage, but argued that below this line it would be harmless. The reply from Under Secretary Pelham rejected these arguments but astonishingly, in the light of Capt. Frederick's conclusions, he added: "that the Board will be prepared to consider any application your clients may make for a licence to dredge at any other part of the coast". At the same time, Sir John convinced the Admiralty to try, unsuccessfully, to persuade the Board to reverse its decision.

On January 22nd Sir John met the fishermen at Torcross, offering them slightly increased compensation if they would withdraw their objections to his operations. The fishermen rejected this offer "by an overwhelming majority", though not unanimously. A possible reason for this division can be found in a (later) memorandum from Frank Mildmay to the Board of Trade, which describes another tactic used by Sir John. At the first public inquiry the fishermen were represented by George Wills, who later changed his mind. Mildmay asks:–

"And who is this George Wills? He is a man whom Sir John Jackson, with a view to propitiating the leading fishermen, has engaged for nominal and non-existent duties at a salary of over £1 a week. Sir John has also hired his house for his agent at a ridiculous rent, as it was originally supposed that Wills controlled all the other fishermen."

Six days after this unsuccessful meeting, taking a lead from Pelham's offer, Sir John signed an Agreement with another landowner to dredge the coast at Strete Gate, some three miles north of Hallsands. Negotiations with the Board were to take several more weeks, as well as another visit from Capt. Frederick, before a licence was granted on May 1st, although Sir John was not prepared to wait that long. From February onwards the fishermen of nearby Strete and Slapton began to complain of damage to moorings; an adjacent landowner protested at damage to her property; and the borough surveyor warned of consequences for the coastal road. It seems nothing had been learned from the mistakes of Hallsands. Fortunately for the people of Slapton and Strete, Sir John decided the samples taken from their coast were unsatisfactory. He gave notice to cancel the Agreement, obtaining the rest of his supplies from a bank off the coast of the Isle of Wight. Did the dredging between February and April proceed with the tacit approval of the Board, or did Sir John take a deliberate decision to defy the law? The direct evidence is inconclusive, but another related incident may provide a clue.

A couple of miles offshore in Start Bay lies Skerries Bank, described by the district council as "a natural breakwater" for the coastal villages. With his licence to dredge at Hallsands removed, Sir John began dredging sand and shingle from this bank almost immediately. This continued unchallenged until some two years later, when the district council complained to Mildmay who, in turn, raised the issue with Sir Francis Hopwood, Permanent Secretary to the Board of Trade. Hopwood initially "doubted the accuracy" of the report, but then wrote to Sir John demanding he stop dredging without permission. In a cleverly worded reply, Sir John agreed to halt the dredging in Start Bay, refused to extend this undertaking to any other areas, and added:–

"it had never occurred to me that it was necessary to obtain the consent of the Crown or anyone else for the removal of material from the Skerries…As a fact, the removal of the sand on the Skerries can have no possible effect on the shore."

Although the map accompanying the original 1896 Agreement has not survived, it is clear from other records that part of Skerries Bank was included in the licence revoked in 1902. Sir John told the Board the full extent of his dredging there had removed 68 barge loads, but later evidence on this from the coastguards to Capt. Frederick was to cast doubt on the accuracy of Sir John's word.

The sea claims its own

During 1902, with no more dredging, the beach began to reform, so the fishermen were able, once again, to leave their boats in front of the village most of the time. Indeed, by August, when figure 20 was taken, the beach at Wilson's Rock had recovered nearly half its fallen level and this, together with sand washing in to fill the excavations, may well have led the more optimistic villagers to believe Sir John's predictions that the sea would indeed repair the damage. However, any such illusions were to disappear with the sand in the first storms of winter. In December the wall in front of the London Inn, rebuilt by Sir John during the previous year, was again attacked by the sea and had to be repaired. Then, in the dark hours of February 26th 1903, at high tide, a storm began to lash the village, which led to waves breaking over houses and to sea water being sent rushing down their chimneys. Isolated and frightened, the villagers stayed up throughout the night, listening for damage and fearing the collapse of any part of their homes. In the small hours of the 27th, as the storm subsided, one of the fishermen, George Stone, ventured out carrying a lantern to check for damage. As he stepped onto the quay in front of the London Inn, the surface gave way beneath him and he fell into a hole, with the tide washing in and out of a chasm below him. Shaken, but unhurt, he pulled himself up and returned home to wait for morning. As day broke, the villagers emerged to see the quay beneath the inn's glass 'teahouse' completely undermined. With access by the front door now unsafe, customers would have to enter through the cellar!

Two nights later the quay at the southern extremity of the village collapsed, taking with it part of the road (see figure 23) and one side of the house shown in figure 24, which was owned by a Miss Ann Trout. The collapse must have occurred in stages as she was able to remove her furniture to her niece's house before the walls were claimed by the sea. The adjoining house, also undermined, was the home of John Gillard, a farm labourer, his wife and two children. A neighbour invited him to move in with his furniture and family, only to find the following night that his house, too, was undermined! This determination and solidarity between neighbours was typical of Hallsands. The

Figure 23: The collapse of the road, March 1903 (*R. Hansford Worth*)

Figure 24: The ruins of Ann Trout's house (*Cookworthy Museum*)

house next to Ann Trout was owned by her kinsman, William, who was also affected, as explained by the civil engineer and geologist R. Hansford Worth:–

"when … the waves were engaged in breaking down the door, Mr Trout, in common with many other householders, took a broom and ejected the floods. Outside the house the waters were ankle deep, sometimes practically knee deep, and the sea after each successful attack on the door endeavoured to set it permanently open by piling shingle against it. But the general opinion at Hallsands appears to be that it's time enough to leave when the house leaves you. The broom won."

A scientific approach

In March 1903 Frank Mildmay again tabled a parliamentary question, calling on the Government to assist the villagers. The President of the Board of Trade, Gerald Balfour, replied promising to investigate, and the incensed men of the village met with parish, district and county councillors in Hallsands' Reading Room to demand action. During this meeting, which took place on the 9th, Edward Windeatt (Mildmay's agent) "made a lengthy speech in favour of the fishermen's immediate compensation", while Revd. Fritzel, vicar of Stokenham and chairman of the parish council, proposed that all the villagers present sign a memorial to be sent to Frank Mildmay. Sensing the urgency of the situation, Mildmay wrote to the Board the same day, enclosing the memorial and resolutions of support from all three councils.

At around this time, as pressure was growing on the Government for some kind of compensation, Mildmay and his supporters decided they would need their own professional advisor. They chose Richard Hansford Worth, the civil engineer and geologist mentioned above, who was to act (mainly unpaid) as the villagers' advisor for years to come. Like his father, R. N. Worth, engineer, geologist and author of *History of Plymouth*, Worth was a man of wide interests and expertise. Apart from his work as an engineer, he became one of the leading authorities of the time on the archaeology of Dartmoor. Always the gentleman, although not one to "suffer fools gladly", he was remembered by friends as "the last of that vanished race of Victorian antiquaries, the like of which we shall not see again". His teenage diaries reveal an obsession with sailing and fishing, which may help to explain his empathy for the people of Hallsands. A future secretary of the Devonshire Association for the Advancement of Science, Literature and Art, his prolific writings for the Association include three papers on the events at Hallsands.

Figure 25: Richard Hansford Worth (*Torquay Museum*)

The earliest of these, published in 1904, contain the first scientific analysis of cause and effect of the changing beach levels along Start Bay. In examining the composition of the beaches, Worth was developing the work of his late father who had studied Slapton Sands for a paper to the Association twelve

31

years earlier. Worth's research showed the beach at Hallsands to be composed mainly of flints and other rock "of undoubtedly foreign origin that is not derivable from the adjacent cliffs". Some of this material had originated on Dartmoor at a time, Worth deduced, when the level of the land had been higher (in fact, the main difference was lower sea levels during the last ice age). Given its ancient source, he concluded "any loss caused by the removal of a portion of the shingle must under present conditions be permanent". He later estimated the shingle removed was equal to at least 600 loads of dredgers, like the one shown in figure 15 above. Playing down any evidence of past variations, he emphasised the stability of the beach over the centuries before the arrival of the dredgers. Although some later researchers have questioned this stability, few have argued with his main conclusion. As Derek Mottershead explains in *Classic Landforms of the South Devon Coast:*–

"In the light of information now available on the nature of Start Bay, and of modern understanding of coastal processes, there can be little doubt that the destruction of South Hallsands was an inevitable consequence of the removal of shingle."

The fight to save the village

On March 15th 1903 the *Western Morning News*, another Plymouth-based newspaper, reported on a visit by Frank Mildmay to Hallsands. Addressing a meeting of fishermen in the Reading Room, he expressed his shock at the scale of the dilapidation that he had just seen, saying the President of the Board of Trade had clearly been "misinformed" when he told Parliament "since the dredging stopped the beach had remade". The fishermen then warned him of the dangers of the Skerries Bank dredging (which had not yet been halted). Some also suggested the village should be rebuilt on safer ground, although "several fishermen whose houses were damaged did not approve of this". Mildmay left, promising to fight for just compensation, and was "heartily cheered on driving off".

On March 19th he wrote again to Balfour, saying: "I have a telegram this evening to the effect that another house at Hallsands has fallen". Doubting moral arguments alone would convince him, he warned the president: "It will play the very devil with my constituency from the political point of view if the Board of Trade do not recognise what is so obviously their duty" (Mildmay's Unionist coalition was still in Government). Four days later he sent a further letter, enclosing the first of Worth's reports; then finally, on March 24th, Capt. Frederick visited Hallsands for another inspection. Echoing Worth's report, he confirmed: "several houses have been so considerably damaged that they are no longer safe to live in, and will probably collapse with the first strong wind…". Interviewing witnesses and examining old ordnance survey maps also convinced him that natural forces had caused the beach to fall in about 1885 and recover by 1897. (A comparison between figure 26 and figure 4 above confirms this – note the shingle bank on which the boats are resting in figure 4, and Wilson's Rock, which was prominent in 1885 but barely visible in 1894.) This observation was to have a significant influence on the Board's attitude to future claims for assistance, although Capt. Frederick himself concluded:–

"...in spite of these great changes wrought by natural causes I have no hesitation in saying that in my opinion the dredging operations...must have contributed in no small degree to the disasters which have lately occurred."

Figure 26: The beach was low due to natural causes in 1885 (*J. Amery*)

Under pressure from Mildmay, in April 1903, the Board of Trade applied to the Treasury for £500, which Sir John Jackson agreed to match. This offer of £1,000 (worth around £70,000 at today's prices) was intended to compensate those who had lost their homes and to pay for new sea defences. It was conditional on the signature of every villager, each accepting the payment as final settlement whatever damage might occur in the future. At a public meeting on April 29th a majority voted to accept, but without the signatures of the others no work could commence.

Hansford Worth, now working free of charge for the villagers, invited several companies to tender for the construction of new sea walls. A few days later he confirmed what many had suspected – that the offer was inadequate. The lowest tender was £1,064, leaving nothing to repair or replace the houses damaged or destroyed by the sea. The villagers and their supporters were faced with a terrible dilemma. Holding out for more realistic compensation would delay the start of the work, while the scale of the damage was increasing with every storm. It took the altruism and "sense of responsibility" of Frank Mildmay to break the impasse with a personal guarantee of up to £1,500, enabling Worth to start while negotiations continued.

The work was beset with problems from the beginning, as Worth was to report to the Devon Sea Fisheries Committee:–

"Not one wall has been constructed that has not within a very few days of its completion received the full brunt of a heavy sea long before the concrete could acquire anything approaching its ultimate solidity."

A ship carrying limestone was wrecked on the nearby coast, disrupting his supply and increasing his costs still further. He also admitted that:–

"The sea wall is a structure in the design of which economy has exercised a controlling influence…it was clearly a case of light walls or nothing."

Nonetheless, with only the southern stretch completed, they were still to show their value in the first storms of autumn: "All the villagers are united in the belief that it was the new wall which saved the [southern] end of the village in the great gale of Sunday night", stated the *Western Morning News* on September 23rd 1903. Elsewhere, the consequences were more serious, as reported in the same article:–

"On Saturday the tide was exceptionally high and some resolved to wait up all night and keep watch. Nothing beyond the moaning of the wind, the roaring of the seas, and the beating of small stones upon the window panes disturbed the tranquillity of the night. At five o'clock on Sunday morning, however, there commenced the first equinoctial gale of the season, accompanied by a growing spring tide. It brought the sea far beyond its usual mark, sending spray into the narrow thoroughfare. The wind increased during the day, making an exceedingly heavy surf roll. Heavy breakers rolled continuously between 5 a.m. and 7.30 p.m. and cleared away the foundations of that portion of the London Inn which suffered so severely in the spring, causing it to collapse with startling rapidity. This section of the building comprised a cellar, kitchen, bedroom and loft, used as a store for fishermen.

The story of the catastrophe is, perhaps, best told in the words of Mr George Lobb, the unfortunate landlord of the London Inn. He said: 'When the greenhouse collapsed two coastguardsmen and two fishermen came to assist me to remove the things in the bedroom. While we were in the room the roof came down upon us, and we all had a narrow escape. Then the gable gave way, tearing away the stove and nearly blinding us with dust. It was with the greatest difficulty that we grasped things to prevent us from falling into the surf. My wife also had a very narrow escape. We had arranged to have tea, as usual in the kitchen. Mrs Lobb was sitting down when the wall gave way, but not in her customary place, otherwise she would have certainly fallen and perished in the surf. We hurriedly removed all articles of furniture, and had just got out the last, when the whole pile went like a pack of cards. The noise and the dust was bewildering, the latter enveloping the assistants and myself. I heard the bystanders shout 'What has become of the men?'"

With the help of the contractors' foreman, Mr Lobb was able to extricate himself and his wife without injury, but as the villagers ventured out the following morning they were confronted with the partial collapse of the inn and the old quay walls.

Figure 27: The London Inn after the storms of September 1903 (*Cookworthy Museum*)

Several visitors to Hallsands at around this time remarked on the stoicism, or even indifference, of the villagers towards their situation. Hansford Worth complained that fishermen idling in bad weather would wander the beach searching for coins rather than help his contractors. Another reporter from the *Western Daily Mercury* commented:–

"Extraordinary as it may appear to the reader to learn that there is really no excitement whatever in Hallsands, yet it is strictly true. Naturally, there are some anxious ones among the small company; but not a trace of excitement is to be found anywhere. Perhaps it is because the possibilities of the situation are not yet appreciated; yet this cannot be, for yesterday a number of men were discussing the prospects of the whole village being eventually swept away. Or perhaps it is because the inherent fortitude of their race and calling come to their aid, and cause them to observe this outwards show of remarkable calmness. The Hallsander is a study for the psychologist at this moment. The man is in deadly peril – he says so himself – and all the while he goes about his daily task with consummate indifference."

Figure 28: The collapse of the old quay walls, 1903 (*Cookworthy Museum*)

Figure 29: A photo taken in November 1903 from the southern end of the village, showing the new walls nearing completion (*R. Hansford Worth*)

Fiddling while the walls fell

By November 1903 the walls across the southern and central stretches of the village were nearing completion – just as available funds were nearing exhaustion. Urging the Board to increase its offer, Mildmay quoted Hansford Worth's opinion that "without the expenditure of £1,500 on defence works all that has been done before may be of no avail". His plea was supported by the Devon Sea Fisheries Committee, whose chairman commented that, if it had been a mansion instead of poor fishermen's houses, the matter would have been put right long before. The sympathy and support of this committee, however, were not reciprocated by the district council, which became involved again as the roads to and through the village continued to deteriorate (the collapse of the old quay wall had left a cavity next to the London Inn extending as far as the crumbling road).

Charged with replacing the wall, and running short of funds, Worth appealed to the district council to help by infilling the cavity behind it. Several members appreciated the need to act quickly, but the majority preferred to appoint a committee to visit the site and report back. So began another round of procrastination.

Surveying the extent of the chasm, the committee decided to refer it back to the full council: the following exchange illustrates the attitudes of the members:–

Mr P. Cole:	protested against the council doing anything on private property. The sole duty of the council was to keep up their road, for which a retaining wall should be built.
Chairman (Adams):	presumed that the council wished to assist all it possibly could, so as to protect the village.
Mr Prettejohn (a local member):	You must protect the sea wall.
Mr Cole:	The sea wall will stand by itself right enough and for a hundred years.
Parish Clerk:	Mr Worth is afraid.
Mr Cole:	After the filling is done, the owner of the London Inn might come and claim the land... I object to doing work on private property at the expense of the ratepayers.

Baulking at the estimated cost of £30, they decided to appoint another, larger committee and to invite Mrs Spital, now the owner of the inn, to attend a meeting. (Following the collapse of most of the inn, the tenant, Mr Lobb, had moved into lodgings, auctioning his furniture "at considerable loss to the owner". A makeshift bar was operating from an old stable block of the inn.)

On November 25th 1903 Mrs Spital was summoned by the district council to

Figure 30: Wilson's Rock, July 1903 (*R. Hansford Worth*)

Figure 31: By December 1903 the Beesands road above these cliffs was crumbling (*R. Hansford Worth*)

the Reading Room, packed with councillors and observers. This must have been an intimidating setting for the elderly widow, and, sensing his advantage, the chairman pressed her for a commitment to contribute £15 (around £1,000 at today's prices), half the estimated cost of filling the cavity. She responded by saying "those who caused the damage should pay for it", to which he replied: "The council is not responsible for the action of the sea, and you will find it difficult to get compensation from Sir John Jackson".

Resisting the pressure to make an immediate commitment, she left the meeting promising to respond by the following week. Two weeks later Mrs Spital's daughter replied to the council, saying: "my mother has instructed me to inform you she has decided not to contribute". This infuriated the chairman, who objected to a suggestion that the council express sympathy for her losses. Mrs Spital, he claimed "had treated the council very badly". Her letter "savoured very much of a 'try on'". As they were later to discover, the feisty Mrs Spital was considering an alternative plan of her own.

Meanwhile, Frank Mildmay, still negotiating with the Board of Trade, read with frustration the newspaper reports of this deadlock. Writing to the council that "every day's delay is an additional damage to the village", he offered to pay the disputed £15 himself. At the same time the sea wall contractor (who must also have been exasperated by the council's attitude) made a once only offer to carry out the work for just £15. Several of the councillors, however, argued that the job should be put out to tender, hoping to reduce the cost (and delay the work) still further. By a vote of six to five they finally agreed to accept the contractor's offer, but by this time the winter storms had already struck!

Figure 32: The Logins' cottages before the dredging (foreground) (*Fred Lynn*)

Outside the protection of the new walls, it was the turn of the northern end of the village to suffer in the gales of December 12th 1903. The families of Robert and William Login were tenants in two of the three cottages shown in figure 32, when, around midnight, a raging sea first demolished the quay in front of their houses and then the front walls of the dwellings. In the cold and dark the occupants carried as much as they could of their furniture across the disintegrating quay to the Reading Room, where they found refuge for the night. On the following day Robert Login, his wife and son moved back into the two rooms which were not directly open to the elements, while William Login, together with his wife and seven children, were taken in by his fishing partner, Mr Lynn, whose own home was described as "very small". It is not recorded how long Robert's family continued to live in the dilapidated house, but by March 1904 all that remained of the three cottages were the ruins shown in figure 33.

Figure 33: The ruins of the Logins' cottages after March 1904 (*Cookworthy Museum*)

The unusual house built into the rock beside them survived, but compare the height of the steps in figure 34 with figure 1 above. Describing a journey to reach the houses at the northern end of the village, the *Western Morning News'* reporter explained:–

"A 30 ft ladder has to be descended to the beach, ending in a walk along the foreshore. This communication is only available at low water. The difficulty of

Figure 34: The Barber family, northernmost house, 1904 or later
(*Fred Lynn*)

the villagers of this part of the hamlet may be imagined when it is realised that all domestic necessaries have to be brought to the houses along the way described. Should the inhabitants of any cottage be caught in this portion when a gale is on, one shudders at the result. The only possible escape would be a rope let down from the top of the cliffs immediately to the rear."

Like most of Hallsands' moments of crisis, when the storms returned on March 5th it was again in darkness. The last sections of the old quay, owned by Kingsbridge Rural District Council, collapsed along with five more houses. One of these (figure 35) belonged to a widow from the unfortunate Login family, now homeless at the age of 70. Another was occupied by Ann Trout, aged 76, as her neighbour described to the *Western Morning News*:–

"About 4.30 a.m. on Saturday morning we were awakened by the roaring of

Figure 35: The ruins of Mrs Login's house, 1904 (*Westcountry Studies Library*)

Figure 36: The severed road, 1904 (*Fred Lynn*)

the sea...[it] came right into the bedroom windows, saturated our bedding and most of our furniture. We lost no time in clearing this out; but our principal difficulty was with Anne Trout. We let her stay in the house until the last, but feeble as she was, she had to go. The sea now commenced to rip the thatch off the roof, and the water got so great that we had to bore holes in...the side of the wall for it to escape into the sea."

The chasm in front of the ruins now severed Hallsands' only street, making the temporary wooden bridge the only means of access to most of the village. All this occurred close to the wall which had taken the district council so long to backfill, causing one reporter to comment that: "had that wall been promptly rebuilt, the cottage at the back of it would have been saved", and another to write:–

"Kingsbridge Rural District Council will find themselves put to more expense than if they had filled up the hole betimes in addition to what they will lose in rates on the destroyed property."

Figure 37: The London Inn was further damaged in March 1904 (*Cookworthy Museum*)

Roads and obstacles to a settlement

Behind these terrible scenes the Board of Trade was now preparing to respond to Mildmay's demands. Permanent Secretary Hopwood met Sir John Jackson in November 1903, reporting that he was, "very indisposed to give more". Around the same time the Board approached the Treasury for approval to increase the size of its compensation. To ease the negotiations Mildmay had offered to make a personal contribution of £250, worth around £18,000 at today's prices. To this, in January 1904, the Government offered to add £1,000 (effectively refunding the royalties received from the dredging) and Sir John £750. The payment would be made to Mildmay, "whose receipt would be conclusive and binding on each and every one of them". However, Mildmay was unhappy with this suggestion, replying that he was "unable to say the proposed sum would enable satisfactory settlement". He pointed out it would leave only £300 to compensate those who had lost their homes. Costs were escalating with the growing dilapidation; it was, as Worth put it, "the whole history of unready money and an ever ready sea". Despite his reservations, Mildmay sent an open letter to the *Western Morning News* inviting the villagers to consider the Board's offer, doubting it would be improved.

Unconvinced, the villagers were still resolved not to sign when Capt. Frederick again visited Hallsands on February 22nd. Quoting Revd. Fritzel's estimate of eighteen houses needing repairs of £1,400, his report implied the increased offer was still inadequate. He confirmed the obvious – that the beach at Hallsands had now reached its lowest ever level, observing that the apparent recovery of the beach to the north of the village had failed to withstand the storms of that winter. This, he concluded: "points in my opinion to the

Figure 38: Wilson's Rock, 1904 (*R. Hansford Worth*)

probability of other causes besides the dredging operations...the unfortunate succession of heavy gales...must be regarded as in large measure the important factor". Unlike Hansford Worth, Capt. Frederick was no expert geologist, but his layman's opinion was to prove useful to the Board and the Treasury. Although he probably never saw this confidential report, Worth was scathing of those who advanced this explanation, comparing it to a man who drops a lighted match in a munitions factory and blames the ensuing disaster on an "unfortunate local concentration of high explosive".

Despite the potential excuse offered by the report, Balfour went to see Sir John personally, playing, no doubt, on his political ambitions to extract a commitment of £1,250. The Government's offer, too, was doubled to £2,000, making a total of £3,500 after including Mildmay's £250. As before, the offer was made without admitting liability and was conditional on every householder signing acceptance that this was the final settlement. In early April, when Mildmay obtained the signatures of all bar one of the householders, they may have believed relief was imminent. Their hopes were to prove premature.

The one person refusing to sign was Mrs Spital, who was now threatening legal action against Sir John. Concerned that she might scupper the whole agreement, Mildmay wrote to Balfour asking, "is it not possible to ignore her?". She was, he believed, "a housekeeper, an uneducated woman and has no resources to go to law". She was to prove him wrong, as her solicitors issued a writ against Sir John and a witness subpoena to Capt. Frederick requiring him to produce a copy of his 1901 report. Ultimately it was Sir John's solicitors who supplied this to the Court, much to the annoyance of the solicitor to the Board. Had Sir John informed them of his intention, he wrote to Hopwood, they would have "claimed privilege", as "there are several things in it that one would rather were not made public". This secrecy was to influence events at Hallsands for decades to come, distorting accounts of the disaster some seventy years later.

In March 1904, with the Board's solicitors still quibbling over the precise wording of the villagers' declaration, the *Western Morning News* launched a relief fund for Hallsands which went on to attract donations from shocked readers across the county. Among them were members of the Mannamead Amateur Dramatic Club, who staged two performances of *A Double Wedding* and contributed £2 2s, and also an anonymous fisherman, who spoke for many when he said:–

"Those of us who sleep warm and dry in their beds every night will perhaps think of these poor people driven out of house and home, and although times are bad with many I feel sure few will grudge a trifle towards helping them."

He enclosed a donation of £10, worth around £700 at today's prices.

By June 6th the appeal had raised £631, to be administered by four trustees: Frank Mildmay, Revd. Fritzel, Hansford Worth and County Councillor Holdsworth. Despite the local landowners' attitude, "as one of business rather than sentiment", a site was eventually found for four new houses on the cliff top beside the Bible Christian Chapel. The 'Western Morning News houses', as they became known, still stand today, a few feet from the edge of the receding cliffs.

Figure 39: The Western Morning News houses today

The *Western Morning News* had a particular reason for closing its appeal on June 6th because five days later the writ was served for a parliamentary by-election in Devonport, where the Unionist candidate was to be Sir John Jackson. Violently pro-Unionist and anti-Radical, they described Sir John in a 'Sketch of the Candidate' as "one of the keenest as well as the most upright of business men". Moreover, for a few weeks all mention of Hallsands disappeared from the columns of the newspaper, enabling a journalist to praise, without irony, Sir John's "munificent gift" of £5,000 to Edinburgh University on the same day as the election was called. His role in the Hallsands collapse does not seem to have figured as an election issue, but when a heckler accused him of discharging men because they wanted trades union pay, the *Western Morning News* approvingly reported his reply:–

"If I were within a foot of you and you told me I was not charitable to the poor, I would do with you what I said last night – I would pretty nearly ring the breath out of you (applause and uproar)."

This robust campaigning style evidently did not impress the voters of Devonport as they elected his opponent, the Radical Liberal John Benn (grandfather of Tony Benn). [The *Western Morning News*, which actively supported the fishermen at other times, has proved a useful source for more recent writers, and may have influenced some in their attitude towards Sir John. In the 1984 booklet *Hallsands, a Pictorial History*, Tanner and Walsh echo the *Western Morning News* in describing Sir John as "a businessman accountable to his shareholders...he appears to have always acted openly". In fact, Sir John and his family owned 90% of the shares in Sir John Jackson Ltd.]

The election over, Sir John's solicitors finally settled Mrs Spital's claim out of court with a payment of £500 plus costs, a satisfactory settlement in comparison to the others. For this he extracted another concession from the Board, reducing his contribution to the general compensation fund by £250, bringing the total down to £3,250, which again appeared less than adequate.

In September the male householders were called to sign another declaration which included the words demanded by the Treasury: "full and final settlement of all claims direct and indirect" and "as far as Sir John Jackson is concerned, it is given purely as a matter of good feeling". Twelve shaky signatures and six crosses mark the fishermen's acceptance of these unequal terms.

In October 1904, as the autumn storms were again attacking the village, Sir Francis Hopwood wrote back to Mildmay, acknowledging receipt of the declaration and making a new suggestion. The villagers had two options, he said: to repair the houses behind new walls or to abandon them, using the money to rebuild further inland. After the storms of that spring, several of the fishermen, in their despair, had already suggested to the press that this would be a better option. Hindsight has confirmed the good sense of this alternative, but, with over £1,000 already spent on the new walls, Mildmay was forced to reply with the words: "I can't put this to them – the grant is insufficient".

At the same time the Board introduced another obstacle. Outraged at the suggestion of any cost falling on the rates, the district council was threatening legal action against Sir John, who responded by demanding that "the fishermen should put the road in repair as part of the consideration for payment". Faced with another demand on the meagre grant, Mildmay replied: "I am bound to say that it appears to me to be the refinement of cruelty to interpose these fresh obstacles to this settlement while the fishermen themselves are as yet defenceless against the winter gales". Extracting an offer of £50 from Sir John (as always, conditional on the council's renunciation of any future claims), Mildmay again offered to match this sum out of his own pocket. But the councillors were still not satisfied, deciding eventually to send their chairman, Mr Willing, to negotiate directly with Sir John.

On November 18th Mildmay, Sir John, Willing and Hopwood met in London. With no more money available from the Treasury, Hopwood persuaded Mildmay and a reluctant Sir John to double their contributions, but Willing still held out for a further £50. With no agreement reached, Sir John announced he had to "leave for the country". What happened next is not recorded, but by December 4th Sir John had paid the council the £250 that they were demanding and finally, four years after the first houses had succumbed to the sea, Mildmay received the compensation cheque (excluding his own contribution) for £3,000.

Figure 40: The disputed section of road (*Cookworthy Museum*)

Calm between the storms

In September 1905 Sir Francis Hopwood visited Hallsands at the request of Balfour and the Treasury, who wanted to know, "how far Hallsands fishermen had expended the money received". He replied:–

"The seawalls have been completed and I understand materially strengthened. They appeared to me to be much more substantial than when I saw part of the work on a former occasion, and to be sound in every respect. The second tier of cottages is repaired, the occupants having made up their minds to rely upon the stability of the sea defences. The front tier of cottages, including the Inn will remain as they were – in a state of ruin – and the inhabitants have built at the top of the cliff rather more to the East some fairly substantial and roomy brick houses [the Western Morning News houses] …"

Referring to houses at the northern end of the village, he wrote:–

"It appears to me to be clear that the fishermen have not expended, by any

Figure 41: August 1906. Note the Western Morning News houses to the far right (*R. Hansford Worth*)

means, the whole of the monies they received, and I can only hope that those who have repaired the cottages below the cliff and are living in them, have put money by to meet further disaster if it falls upon them."

His belief that the grant would leave a surplus was mistaken; it was spent as follows:–

	£	s	d
Sea walls	1,720	17	6
Owners of 6 demolished houses	390	0	0
Repairs to remaining houses	778	7	6
Damage to furniture etc.	159	10	0
Damage to boats and loss of fishing gear	193	15	0
Expenses	7	10	0
TOTAL	3,250	0	0

Figure 42: Behind the walls life returned to a kind of normality (*Fred Lynn*)

Six owners were paid an average of £65 for the total loss of their homes, which was far from generous – a few years earlier Hallsands cottages had been selling for over £100. Owners of the other cottages "in a state of ruin" were compensated at even lower levels from the repairs budget. Ultimately, some of the buildings on the seaward side of the road, including the London Inn, were rebuilt, although by 1917 only twenty-five of the original thirty-seven houses remained occupied. By choice or necessity, many of the villagers had left Hallsands by then.

The expenses total included £2 5s for Hansford Worth, who refused to accept any more payment for his years of work. Behind his walls, life at Hallsands returned to a kind of normality. The fishermen continued their work, faced with a steep haul up the new slipways at the end of every day. And, apart from Worth's occasional talks, newspapers and official files hardly refer to the village for over a decade.

Figure 43: Boats had to be hauled up and down this slipway (*Fred Lynn*)

When war broke out in 1914 the fishermen's experience of the sea made them ideal recruits for the Royal Navy. With his distinguished service in the Boer War, and fluency in French, Mildmay was allowed to enlist at the age of 53. Rising to the rank of Lt. Colonel, he continued his urgent constituency work under difficult conditions from the headquarters of VII Corps in France. Sir John Jackson, meanwhile, responded to the declaration of war by offering: "in case any works of hasty defence were urgently required, to place at Lord Kitchener's disposal any engineering assistance [he or his Company] was able to give...". The terms of this offer were not clear, although Sir John maintained his motives were purely patriotic.

Many of Hallsands' younger men were away on active service when the first signs of trouble began to appear back home. In January 1915 Mr T. Barber, owner of one of the "cottages below the cliff" (see figure 34 above) whose security Pelham had questioned, wrote to the district council complaining about a cliff fall. Tons of rock had "half filled the foundations" of houses he was building at the northern end of the village. A chartered engineer by profession, he wrote to several public authorities, including this warning to Devon County Council:–

"It is evident that unless steps are taken during the ensuing summer to provide an adequate sea wall right along the front the village will become untenable."

His plans for a second sea wall in front of the first, however, were rejected or ignored. A civil servant at the Board of Trade noted in 1916:–

"Mr Barber is evidently an old man. He has known Hallsands intimately for 62 years and does not like being told what to do. If there was anything in this surely we would have heard from the District Council or from Mr Mildmay…"

'A very sacred memory'

Figure 44: The gales drove the waves, full of shingle, over the sea walls
(*Fred Lynn*)

At high tide on the night of January 26th 1917, a south-easterly gale drove the waves full of shingle over the sea walls and against the houses. Edith Patey, the devout non-conformist quoted above, was aged 17 at the time. In 1970, towards the end of her life, she described what happened next:–

"The windows had all been shuttered and doors securely protected. All the fishermen were over Greenstraight getting their boats all safely put further inland. They each knew what would come on that night of our family experience. Dad came in the back door. So Mum got his tea ready. He only just went in the scullery to wash his hands. Then all of a sudden the walls came toppling down, the floor caved in and Dad had the presence of mind to hold on to the frame of the door, and managed to come across a stone passage which was the centre part of the cottage. The part up over the scullery had completely caved in...We felt like being right in the sea, the roaring waves bouncing over us, the rafters all breaking in. We could see the white waves foaming underneath the floors. The coal house all slipping away, no fires, the sea came down the chimney.

Well Dad calmly knew the safest place we could huddle together. So he put a sail to protect us and moved a few heavy things to support us. To this very day that safe place is still there, where we were all saved. A very sacred memory."

A newspaper reporter interviewed several of the survivors:–

"Some of the people had a terrible experience. In one case there were nine people huddled together in a little house against which the waves were incessantly dashing, and they were expecting every moment that the walls which afforded them shelter would collapse, and that they would be washed away. They had to bore holes in the bedroom floor to let the water down into the kitchen. It was impossible to save anything in the place, or for them to make their escape until the tide went out. One of the fishermen, James Lynn, saw two huge waves crash against his house and knock most of the front of it clean in. The lamp was extinguished, and the people were in utter darkness, but they managed to make their escape by the back door."

Some of the houses on the landward side of the road survived that storm only to succumb the following night. Visiting the village on the 28th, a *Western Daily Mercury* reporter wrote:–

"Coming around the bend of the road in full view of the village a pitiful site confronted me. The scene of destruction can hardly be described. The sea and wind, in playfulness or spite, had wiped out the houses of a happy people in a few hours. The village street had been torn up, and pedestrians had to negotiate great gaping holes. Some cottages had simply collapsed, while of others the front walls had fallen out and the other parts of the structures had tumbled down, shattering much of the furniture inside. It is marvellous how the villagers escaped injury from the falling debris."

By the following morning Old Hallsands was no more and the only buildings untouched were those at the top of the cliffs – the coastguard station, the Western Morning News houses and the chapel. In one respect, it seems, the prayers of the villagers had been answered: not one person was killed or

Figure 45: Sea Scouts helped to salvage possessions from the ruins (*Fred Lynn*)

seriously injured, although twenty-four families were now homeless. At this time of their greatest need, help came from all the surrounding communities. Sea Scouts helped to salvage furniture and possessions from the ruined houses; Harris and Sons, the Kingsbridge grocers, sent four of their staff to help Mrs Mingo, owner of the ruined village shop; the Patey family, like many others, were offered accommodation on a farm, a mile or so inland; and others were taken in by relatives in Beesands and Kingsbridge, or left the area altogether.

Most of the fishing boats and equipment were damaged or destroyed, leaving the fishermen with the immediate problem of how to earn a living. As one of them asked the *Western Daily Mercury* reporter:–

"What are we going to do? We have spent the whole of our lives here fishing. We know no other trade, and we are useless. We have no homes. Much of our furniture is lost. I tell you it's hard, very hard for our wives and families. It's all gone."

The pressure grows

On the Thursday following the collapse, at the suggestion of Hansford Worth and Mrs Mildmay, the *Western Morning News* launched a new disaster relief fund. Rehousing the people of Hallsands was its main aim, although some would be used to repair damage at Beesands and Torcross. "The duty of all Westcountry folk is apparent", it stated, "war or no war – and that is to whet once more the display of generosity they have already shown so handsomely in connection with the innumerable war funds...". Colonel and Mrs Mildmay were the first subscribers, giving £100 and £10 respectively. At a time when the failures of the generals on the Western Front were largely unreported, this example of official negligence closer to home generated public sympathy and outrage. J.P. Goldsmith from Plymouth wrote:–

"Although I share the view with most others that the Government, who permitted contrary to the advice of the inhabitants, the removal of the shingle at Hallsands should now bear the responsibility, yet as a mark of sympathy with the innocent victims who are in immediate need I am happy to enclose £5."

The Devon Sea Fisheries Committee wrote to the Board of Trade calling for "full compensation" and "the construction of works of adequate protection against future damage". The reply from Assistant Secretary Garnham Roper relied predictably on the declaration signed by the householders in 1904. As they had accepted a "full and final payment...neither the Board of Trade nor Sir John Jackson are under any obligation to contribute towards the protection of Hallsands Village against the sea, or to compensate the villagers...". The Committee could apply to the Treasury's Development Fund for sea defence work but "in view of the importance of restricting capital expenditure and economising labour during the war, the Board are of the opinion that no works of this nature should be undertaken at the present time unless they can be shown to be urgently required".

This last suggestion was something of a diversion, as Mildmay pointed out to Junior Minister G. Roberts:–

"...it was not a question of providing new sea defences, since the village was gone, neither were grants available from the Development Fund to reimburse private individuals for loss of property."

Public concern had now spread beyond the immediate area, and it was another Devon M.P., Sir J. Spear, who called for compensation in a parliamentary question on March 7th. The reply from Roberts simply restated the same reasons for rejection. Mildmay had also given notice of a parliamentary question but changed his mind, preferring to 'work on' Roberts behind the scenes. Sensing the hostility of the civil servants, he tried to balance their briefings with a report of his own and one from Hansford Worth. The original licence, Worth explained, set no limits on the removal of shingle from the foreshore, yet it required the dredgers not to "expose the land to encroachment...Did it not occur to either authority", he asked, "that the task set Shylock to take his pound of flesh without spilling blood was no more difficult than the task here set Sir John Jackson?".

This colourful language, which stands out amongst the official papers, did not impress the civil servants, whose comments are pencilled in the margins. Worth's explanations are described as "special pleading" in one. Where he writes that the 1904 grant was insufficient to rebuild the village, a pencil note is added: "This if Sir John Jackson's report is true is a carelessness as to fact which is discreditable. He was offered the whole place for £1,500." It is interesting to consider how this inaccurate anecdote may have influenced the Board's attitude to the question of compensation: "There seems to be no reason why the Board should be held responsible for the failure of the seawalls which were erected by the villagers on their own initiative and on the advice of their own engineer..." wrote Roberts to Mildmay on April 11th. The villagers, he believed, had chosen to build sea walls when they could just as easily have rebuilt the village inland. He also repeated their belief "that the condition of the village was largely due to natural causes, this is supported by the reports made by Capt. Frederick". Stung by the implication that he was to blame, Worth wrote another long letter to the Board. Again, the pencil notes reveal the attitudes of the civil servants:–

"This seems to be interesting only in the information that the sea walls are still standing unharmed, although they have no beach in front of them."

"This letter does not appear to produce any new information...I think no action is necessary."

Figure 46: The sea walls stood for some time after the collapse of the village
(*Cookworthy Museum*)

In his letter to Roberts, Mildmay wrote: "that the position of these homeless families is now quite lamentable... they are crowded into the dwellings of their neighbours". Faced with the severity of their plight, Revd. Parry (the new vicar of Stokenham) made an urgent request to the *Western Morning News* fund for "a small sum to provide temporary homes and household requisites for those who have lost well nigh everything". Meanwhile, in order to escape the overcrowded hospitality of their neighbours, some villagers took their chances in the ruins. Harold and Rhoda Trout, for example, re-roofed and moved into the old shop before the sea washed them out for a second time. In desperation they then made a new home in the loft above the chapel.

Responding to the growing pressure, Albert Stanley, President of the Board of Trade, agreed to meet a deputation that included the leaders of the Devon Sea Fisheries Committee, a director of the *Western Morning News* and six of Devon's M.P.s. (Col. Mildmay was unable to leave his war duties, but sent a letter of support.) The handwritten notes of the meeting, on June 7th, are interspersed between parentheses with the comments of the civil servant taking the minutes, seeking to undermine the arguments of the deputation. E.C. Perry, Chairman of the Sea Fisheries Committee, explained how the fishermen had "foretold" the disaster of Hallsands. They had been given no choice but to sign the Board's legal disclaimer in 1904. Windeatt said: "the requirements of the dispossessed villagers would be met by the erection of 25 cottages costing between £200 and £300 each". At this point the minute-taker added: "this estimate probably covers not only the occupiers of the cottages in existence prior to 1903/4 but also those of the new houses built since that time". In fact, twenty-five of the original homes had been destroyed. Albert Stanley appears to have said little until closing the meeting with an offer, accepted by the deputation, to appoint another inspector for Hallsands' fourth and final inquiry.

An 85-year secret

To chair the inquiry, the Board chose Sir Maurice Fitzmaurice, voluntary chairman of its Canal Control Committee and former President of the Institute of Civil Engineers. Sir Albert had made his commitment without reference to the Treasury, whose approval was now needed to pay Sir Maurice's fee. The request caused alarm amongst the Treasury's civil servants: writing to his superior, Principal A.W. Hurst stated:–

"I really cannot see how this inquiry is going to help us at all. Legally our position is unassailable. The inhabitants accepted a certain sum in 1904 in full satisfaction and have said nothing, so far as we know, since then…Their claim rests very largely now on compassionate grounds and it must be recognised…we are likely to get off much cheaper by making it clear from the outset that this is the way we look at it. For one thing we need only do something for those who have suffered very severely in proportion to their resources. In this way many of the owners of the property will be ruled out…"

His superiors agreed but accepted the Government was now bound by Sir Albert's commitment and, reluctantly, "raised no objection" to the appointment.

Sir Maurice visited Hallsands on September 24th 1917, made his own examinations and heard evidence from the Devon Sea Fisheries Committee, Hansford Worth and several of the homeless fishermen. There was no representative of Sir John Jackson, who later complained that neither he nor his company were invited, although Sir Maurice maintained that they "were given every opportunity" to participate.

The terms of reference required Sir Maurice to assess the extent of the damage and to ascertain whether it would "have been prevented or mitigated if the dredging operations...had not taken place". In the event, his analysis of the causes largely agreed with Hansford Worth's, concluding, "that the damage done at Hallsands is due altogether to the dredging operations of Sir John Jackson Ltd between Hallsands and Beesands".

Rapid inflation had followed the outbreak of war, more than doubling the general price level since the 1904 settlement. Sir Maurice recognised this in his report, recommending that compensation should reflect current costs of rebuilding, around 9d per cubic foot. In all, twenty-five houses had been destroyed plus the Reading Room, which he valued at the same level as a house. A pencil note from a civil servant reads: "I don't see why we should pay for this". In total, he recommended compensation as follows:–

26 buildings	£8,000
Stores and gear	£1,250
Furniture and belongings	£500
Drainage, water supply and roads	£750
	£10,500

In its letter of appointment, the Board asked Sir Maurice to take "into consideration the payment made in 1904 and the fact that some of the houses recently damaged have apparently been built since that date". In fact, the only new buildings were the Western Morning News houses, which were undamaged and not included in the twenty-five for compensation. Sir Maurice's response to this suggestion was clear:–

"I cannot see any reason for taking the payment made in 1904 into consideration, or the fact that some of the houses have been partly rebuilt or repaired since that date."

Apart from the usual "full and final settlement" clause, he recommended only one condition of payment: "that no houses of any kind should be built on the site of Hallsands village". The compensation "should be divided under the supervision of a local committee with a member of the Devon Sea Fisheries Committee as Chairman".

In his conclusions, Sir Maurice referred to the success of Mrs Spital in obtaining £500 through legal action. Valued at "the very moderate sum" of 3d a ton, Sir John Jackson had obtained shingle worth £8,000 (this estimate probably excludes the unknown quantities extracted from Skerries Bank). "In my opinion any compensation paid to the villagers ought to be refunded to the

Board by Sir John Jackson Ltd."

In 1909 Hansford Worth wrote in the *Transactions of the Devonshire Association*:–

"...the beach material at Slapton is still for sale, and may be purchased in cartloads from the local Rural District Council. Is it too much to hope that wiser counsels may yet prevail...?"

One immediate consequence of Sir Maurice's report was the wiser counsel which persuaded the Board to halt coastal dredging at Slapton and at Bridport, in Dorset. In other respects the report angered the Treasury and embarrassed the Board, whose assistant secretary, Garnham Roper, wrote:–

"Despite Sir Maurice Fitzmaurice's report I feel that it is difficult to believe that the village of Hallsands would not have suffered from the exceptionally severe storms of January 1917 had the dredging which took place in 1897-02 never been sanctioned...If the removal of materials for useful works carries with it an obligation to meet for all time claims like these by men who, despite their fears, remained in houses near the shore where they were destroyed 15 years afterwards, it will have a deterrent effect on enterprise."

Figure 47: The northern end of the village after the storm of 1917 (*Fred Lynn*)

In another letter the Lords of the Treasury regretted that "this enquiry was conducted in such a way as could not fail to give rise to the impression amongst the villagers that the final settlement of their claim...arrived at in 1904, was being re-opened".

Financial Secretary (and future Prime Minister) Stanley Baldwin agreed

59

with his assistant secretary, Meiklejohn, who wrote:–

"I have already intimated privately to the Board of Trade that in future, when questions affecting the Exchequer arise, the Treasury will object to the employment of Sir Maurice Fitzmaurice whose sole concern appears to be to make proposals involving the Exchequer in large expenditure."

Inflation and the inadequacy of the 1904 settlement were two factors which the Treasury was reluctant to accept. Meiklejohn continued:–

"As bearing on Sir Maurice Fitzmaurice's figures it may be mentioned that in 1904 we paid £390 compensation for 6 houses totally demolished: i.e. £65 a piece. He suggests £8,000 for 26, or £308 a piece! Fancy valuing fishermen's cottages at about 9d a cu. ft! Good quality houses around London were built at 7d before the War."

Caught between the Treasury and the political pressure for a fair settlement, the Board decided to build a case for a lower level of compensation. A copy was sent to Sir John Jackson, who, the civil servants suggested, "will be able to criticise the statements made in the report". This strategy depended on keeping the report away from the press, the public and people like Col. Mildmay who represented the villagers. Although rumours of its contents eventually reached Mildmay, the report itself remained confidential until some time after the Second World War when it was released with other papers to the Public Record Office, where it remained unnoticed for the rest of the century.

One sympathises with them, but …

In October 1917, nine months after the collapse, Mildmay asked Sir Albert Stanley in the Commons whether he had read a decision following the inquiry. A few weeks later Principal Clerk C. H. Grimshaw wrote to his superiors: "The President, I understand is pressing for a decision today, but it is no fault of Harbours Department that we are not in a position to suggest a decision".

In November, Second Secretary Sir William Marwood called on Sir John Jackson with a copy of the inquiry report, on which his comments and criticisms were invited. On December 19th he replied: "I am of the opinion that the suggested figures for the damages which should be paid, as given by Sir Maurice, are most excessive". He repeated the claim that his solicitor had suggested before the dredging, that he buy the whole village for "£1200 or at the outside £1500". He denied the "puny efforts of Sir John Jackson Ltd" could have caused such a disaster and argued the villagers had already received generous compensation. Without naming a source, he also claimed the sea had destroyed the village once before, "some fifty or sixty years ago". "It seems strange", he concluded, that Sir Maurice had not approached him or his staff, "whose only interest could have been to have put forward the true state of affairs honestly in the interests of the Hallsands fishermen, with whom, so far as I can remember, throughout the whole of our working there we had the most pleasant relations".

On January 3rd Sir John, Sir Maurice and three officials met in Marwood's office at the Board of Trade. Sir John repeated his views on the question of compensation and "declined to contribute further money". By this time the Government's solicitors had advised that legal proceedings against him stood little chance of success. Sir John also revealed the source of his story about the earlier destruction of Hallsands was the same solicitor who had valued the village at £1,500, and who was now dead. Sir John "promised to ascertain... whether the records of the firm bear this out and also whether there is any other evidence bearing on this point". Sir Maurice referred to witness evidence which cast doubt on this story; including a fisherman who had lived at Hallsands for 78 years in 1904 when he swore a statement (in Mrs Spital's legal action) denying any such collapse. It is worth noting here the title deeds of the London Inn, which date back to the 18th century. There is no record of Sir John producing any further evidence, and the Board's officials were forced to conclude that he had failed to make "any sound arguments against the fishermen's claims which were not put before Sir Maurice...".

Despite the misgivings of his officials, Sir Albert Stanley was now convinced of the need to settle the villagers' claims. On February 1st 1918, at his instruction, Marwood wrote to the Treasury with Sir Maurice's report, drawing attention to the recommended £10,500 compensation. "The Board feel they cannot ignore the recommendations", he wrote, without specifically endorsing the figure. The Treasury was not convinced; Assistant Secretary Meiklejohn wrote:–

Figure 48: The ruins of Old Hallsands (*Fred Lynn*)

"If we offer [a grant] at once we shall only be pressed for more – the Hallsands fishermen, as past history shows, are past masters in squeezing. One sympathises with them in the disaster which has overtaken them but a year or more has now elapsed and it is probable that by now they have managed to get homes and a livelihood."

Of Hallsands' pre-war population, a little over half were still living nearby, renting rooms or overcrowding the homes of their neighbours, and some were still fishing. Some had moved away and others, whose names are listed on the war memorial in front of Stokenham Church, no longer needed rehousing. On March 18th the Treasury responded: "My Lords regret that they can see no adequate reason for placing upon the Exchequer any further charge in connection with the case".

An inadequate settlement

Whether troubled by conscience or fear of the Devon M.P.s "waiting to open fire", Sir Albert Stanley refused to accept this rejection, appealing directly to the Chancellor of the Exchequer, Bonar Law:–

"…the matter…has dragged on for so long…I hope you agree that some additional payment should be made to these unfortunate people. Personally I feel they have a bona fide claim notwithstanding the settlement to which they were a party in 1904…"

In May 1918 Stanley met with Law and Baldwin, who finally agreed to a grant of £6,000: the justification for this reduced payment rested on the 1904 settlement and the Board's belief that "natural causes" were partially to blame. The owners of destroyed houses were to be compensated at pre-war prices, roughly half their current value after four years of wartime inflation. The task of assessing the claims and distributing the grant was delegated to the Devon Sea Fisheries Committee, whose clerk, H. Ford, responded to the Board: "they are satisfied that the sum of £6,000 is quite inadequate".

Allocating the grant caused them "considerable trouble" and provoked one owner, Mr J. Barber, to write to the Board rejecting his "absurdly inadequate" award. A schedule of claims from twenty owners in 1919 lists four living at "Hallsands" and ten others at local farms or in the nearby towns of Kingsbridge and Dartmouth. In his letter, Mr Barber explained he had been renting a room in London for ten shillings a week since the collapse. For twenty-eight cottages and four other buildings the Committee paid a total of £2,188, an average of £68 per building. Subtracting payments for furniture and equipment left £3,200 plus £700 from the *Western Morning News* appeal. As in 1904 the Treasury's insistence on precise documents delayed the payments. In the meantime, the cost of building new houses continued to rise.

On June 21st 1919 the Hallsands sub-committee of the Sea Fisheries Committee visited the village to find out:–

1. How many of the dispossessed householders desired to return to Hallsands.
2. How many of these were in a position after receipt of their compensation, to pay the £200 necessary to acquire a house.
3. The views of the local inhabitants on the question of the site for the new village.

Four owners (of eleven cottages) did not intend to return; seven owners definitely wanted to buy thirteen houses (including George Trout, wanting four for his extended family) and three were undecided. At an estimated cost of £400 each, the Committee reckoned it would need to borrow just £260. Its report adds:–

"...this does not prove the adequacy of the grant, as there are certain of the late inhabitants who would return, if they could rent, but they cannot afford to buy: and again, we should strictly have been able to hand these houses to the fishermen without additional cost to them..."

Eventually the owners committed to sixteen houses for which the Committee bought land on higher ground in the Bickerton Valley behind the beach at what is now known as North Hallsands. The owners agreed to leave their compensation invested at 4% interest by the Committee, but the cost of building was rising faster than this.

A housing shortage and growing dissatisfaction with poor housing at the end of the First World War led Prime Minister Lloyd George to promise "a fit country for heroes to live in", popularised as the slogan "homes fit for heroes". The Housing and Town Planning Act of 1919 imposed a duty on every council to assess local need and plan for council housing, with Government subsidies. Some councils refused to co-operate, forcing the Minister of Health to intervene. One of the last to hold out was Kingsbridge Rural District, whose response to the Ministry revealed their usual aversion to spending and referred to another problem which continues to afflict the area today:–

"...this Council in view of the number of houses especially in the coast parishes of the district kept vacant during the greater part of the year for the convenience of summer visitors, and in view of the pressure put on this Council by the Ministry of Health to build houses at great cost to the ratepayers would heartily support any action taken by the Government to make it illegal to keep houses suitable for members of the wage earning classes vacant for many months continuously..."

The Government did not respond to this suggestion but appointed an inspector in November 1920, who recommended the council to plan for forty houses, including twelve at Hallsands. Interestingly, this was the first mention of Hallsands in the council's minutes for many years; the 1917 collapse passing without comment.

Even with a Government subsidy of £260 per house, the Fisheries Committee was projecting a deficit of over £10,000 on the planned development, whilst the council refused even to pay for the drainage. Mildmay wrote to the Board of Trade that it was "an open secret that your own Board of Trade official who held the enquiry placed the just claims considerably higher than £6,000". The reply offered "little hope of the Treasury being prepared to consider a further payment", but volunteered to raise the matter with the Ministry of Health. In turn, they suggested costs could be cut by, for example, replacing the water closets with earth closets.

Following the inspector's report, the land bought by the Committee was transferred to Kingsbridge Rural District to develop for council housing, with the remaining grant offered as a subsidy. The final plans were under consideration by the Housing Commissioner when an economic downturn forced the Government to cut public spending. In June 1921 the Ministry of Health wrote to the Board of Trade saying:–

"In view of the limitation of the number of houses to be erected under the provision of the State-assisted Housing Scheme and the fact that it has been decided for the present to concentrate on the larger industrial areas, it has now been found impossible to allot any houses to meet the requirements of this village."

The last references to Hallsands in the Government papers are a series of handwritten notes from Treasury officials such as this:–

"I don't see why Board of Trade are now bothering about this; they and Office of Woods should on info. available stand entirely aside.

G. H. Wright 15/8"

By August 1922 the Fisheries Committee admitted defeat and, with the help of a loan of £3,623 from the Public Works Loan Board, began work on a reduced development of just ten houses. Named Fordworth Cottages in honour of H. Ford and Hansford Worth, they were transferred to the newly-formed Hallsands Housing Society. Their foundation stone was laid by E. C. Perry, Chairman of the Fisheries Committee, at a ceremony in April 1923. Hansford Worth spoke of the Committee's work as "a fight against injustice" and Windeatt "expressed the hope that the fishermen would soon own their own houses". A couple of fishermen presented a basket "containing huge crabs and a lobster to members of the committee as a token of appreciation for all that had been done". The gifts were "received with genuine pleasure" but carried off, still alive "with decided caution".

By July 1924 the houses were ready for occupation but, at six shillings a week, they were expensive compared to typical private rents of one to three shillings. At first none of the fishermen applied, forcing the Committee to consider offering them to outsiders, but eventually ten of the original families, including the Trouts, the Lynns and the Prettejohns, became the first tenants. Windeatt's hope was not to be fulfilled – the former homeowners would pay rent for the rest of their lives.

Figure 49: Fordworth Cottages under construction (*Devon Record Office*)

What became of them?

In 1914, shortly after the outbreak of war, the War Office took up Sir John Jackson's offer of "assistance" with a request to build huts for British troops. Although the terms of his offer were not specific, the suggestion, which he later confirmed, was to work like many other firms for expenses only. A few days later, a much larger contract was identified – to build huts for troops from the colonies. General Sir George Scott-Moncrieff, Director of Works, originally intended to employ a Canadian company but, according to a parliamentary report, the Chief Engineer of the Southern Command "had known Sir John Jackson at Plymouth and wished him to have the work". Sir John went to see the general and offered to take the larger contract for 5% commission plus 1.5% "establishment expenses". Scott-Moncrieff considered these commissions too high, but it was agreed to defer the question of payment until the work was complete.

In January 1915 the Marquess of Bath and three Justices of the Peace complained to the War Office that Sir John's work was "not adequate to the money paid". Sir John responded by "personally dismissing" some of his workforce, who he referred to as "idlers". The work complete, the War Office acceded to most of Sir John's demands, paying him £800,000 in commission and expenses (over £30 million at today's prices).

Profiteering was an emotive political issue at the time; according to Robert Graves, soldiers in the trenches regarded much of the population back home in a hierarchy of contempt, starting with staff officers "down to the detested grades of journalists, profiteers... and members of the Government". When the parliamentary Public Accounts Committee found that Sir John, an M.P. of the ruling coalition, had benefited from "extortionate" payments it became headline news. Insulted, Sir John wrote to the War Office demanding an independent judicial inquiry. This last inquiry into Sir John's activities broadly agreed with the parliamentary committee, concluding:–

"His career as a successful contractor making large profits in work requiring large capital and with risks which fortunately seem never in his case to have led to disaster, seems to have given him an altogether inflated idea of the market value of the services of his firm when rendered under different circumstances which involved no risk whatever..."

His reputation "besmirched", Sir John retired from parliament in 1918 and died a year later, at the age of 68, from heart failure.

Frank Mildmay continued as M.P. for Totnes until his ennoblement as Lord Mildmay of Flete in 1922. He died in 1947, aged 85, when simultaneous funerals were held in London, Holbeton in Devon and Shoreham in Kent. A

Figure 50: Lord Mildmay of Flete
and his family (*Anthony Mildmay-White*)

Figure 51: Ella (left) and Patience Trout (*By kind permission of Gill Norman*)

Shoreham villager remembered him as "a man of gentle charm and kindly manner, who had cared for those living and working there during a hard and depressing period of the twentieth century".

Richard Hansford Worth also survived into his eighties, and is remembered today as the author of *Worth's Dartmoor*. He received several awards during his lifetime, including a gold medal from the Royal Geological Society of Cornwall, but his proudest possession was a small silver tobacco box inscribed: 'R. Hansford Worth. A simple token of gratitude from Hallsands, March 1905'.

The families made homeless by the collapse included a widow, Eliza Trout, and her four daughters. They moved to nearby Bickerton during the negotiations, from where the two elder daughters continued to fish. When a cargo ship was hit by a German submarine on September 8th 1917, Ella Trout rowed out to rescue the sole survivor, risking her own life. For this act she was awarded an O.B.E. and a gift of £5 (described as "paltry" in the press) by the Board of Trade. It was also widely reported that the family of the rescued man paid her a reward, and although members of the Trout family have denied this, the sisters later raised enough money to build a guesthouse on the cliffs overlooking the ruined village. It still operates to this day as Trouts Holiday Apartments, and is a welcome place of refreshment along the coast path.

Organised fishing continued from the new village of North Hallsands until 1974, when the Southampton crab smack ceased its weekly visits. The Hallsands Housing Society built two more houses in 1932, finally clearing its debts in the late 1990s. Today, the houses are still offered at modest rents to local people, although local fishermen, the first priority, are becoming more difficult to find.

Figure 52: Trout's Hotel in the 1950s (*Gill Norman*)

Still waiting for justice

We will never know how long Old Hallsands would have survived without the dredging, or whether natural causes would have intervened before our times of climate change and rising sea levels. But there is little doubt the collapse of the village was a direct consequence of the removal of its beach. By suppressing Sir Maurice Fitzmaurice's report, the Government concealed the weakness in its arguments for reduced compensation. Had the other villagers been able to take legal action, like Mrs Spital, the compensation awarded in 1904 would have been greater and might have enabled the rebuilding of the village. As it was, when the decision was made to start work on sea walls, houses were already collapsing and the offer from Sir John and the Board only amounted to £1,000. The error of that decision is hardly justification for the Government's refusal to rehouse all the victims. Wartime constraints on public spending would have been a strong argument in 1918, but no such excuse can be made today.

The replacement of thirty-seven houses with sixteen is now a matter of history, but the failure to provide communal facilities continues to afflict the 'new' village of North Hallsands. The owner of the Reading Room, scene of so many of Hallsands' dramatic moments, was paid just £45 in 1919 (worth around £1,500 at today's prices) and no replacement was ever built. The Hallsands Hotel, built to replace the London Inn, survived until the end of the century, when its closure removed the only meeting place in the village.

Today, a letterbox and a payphone are the only public facilities for a population, excluding second homes, of thirty-three adults and around twenty children.

The difference between Sir Maurice's recommendation and the actual payment in 1919 amounted to £4,500. Increased in line with general prices (property values have increased far more), this would now be worth £150,000 – a debt which the Department of Trade and Industry, successor to the Board of Trade, still owes to the community of Hallsands.

* * * * *

Sources

The Cookworthy Museum of Rural Life in Kingsbridge supplied many of the photographs and other documents, including eyewitness accounts. I have deposited a copy of most of my source documents with the Museum, which offers a research service. Copies of some of the original documents (and study exercises for schools) can also be seen on: www.hallsands.org.uk.

Other non-published sources include: Public Records Office (BT 297/573, 574, 579, T161/69), Devon Records Office (including minutes of Kingsbridge Rural District Council and records of Devon Sea Fisheries Committee), Plymouth Records Office (1747/6, 1069/4) and Stokenham Parish Council minutes.

Published sources include: *Transactions of the Devonshire Association* (1904, 1909 and 1923), Hansard (various), *Geographical Journal* 1961 CXXVII Part 1, The *Western Morning News*, *Western Evening Herald* and *Western Daily Mercury* (all held in Plymouth Library), *Transactions of the Plymouth Institution* (Vol.22), *A Living from the Sea* (Dickinson, M. (ed.)), *Goodbye to All That* (Graves, G.), *Classic Landforms of the South Devon Coast* (Mottershead, D.), *A Poor Man's House* (Reynolds, S.), *Hallsands a Pictorial History* (Tanner, K. & Walsh, P.), and *Shoreham a Village in Kent* (White, M. & Saynor, J.).

Acknowledgements

Fred Lynn, who was born in Hallsands, remembers playing amongst the ruins as a child. His grandfathers, James Lynn and George Trout, shown in figure 7, were amongst the first tenants of Fordworth Cottages, where Fred still lives today. He developed a fascination with the old village, collecting articles and photographs, several of which are used in this book.

Thanks also to: Cookworthy Museum, Devon Records Office & Westcountry Studies Library, Exeter University Library, Plymouth Records Office & Local Studies Library, Plymouth Museum, Public Records Office, Stokenham Parish Council, Torquay Museum.

Robert Cattell, Gill Claydon, Anthony Mildmay-White, Gill Norman, Jim Trout, Guy Pannell.

Index

The Author

Steve Melia is a novelist, environmental campaigner and former Liberal Democrat parliamentary candidate, from South Brent in Devon. As founder member of SHARD (South Hams Against Rural Destruction), he has appeared regularly on TV and radio across the Westcountry. His first novel, *Sins of the Fathers,* is due to be published by Pegasus Elliot MacKenzie in the summer of 2002.

Originally, he was researching the Hallsands story as background for another novel, when he found the suppressed report of the 1918 public inquiry lying unnoticed in the Public Records Office, in Kew. Intrigued, he decided to widen his search to reveal how much of the true story had never been told. His short stories and more information can be found on: www.stevemelia.co.uk.

Steve Melia